THE STAINED-GLASS WINDOWS

OF CHAGALL

1957-1970

ROBERT MARTEAU

THE STAINED-GLASS WINDOWS OF CHAGALL

1957-1970

WITH AN AFTERWORD BY CHARLES MARQ

TUDOR PUBLISHING COMPANY
NEW YORK

759.7
M

CONTENTS

INTRODUCTION 9

NOTRE DAME DE TOUTE GRACE CHURCH, PLATEAU D'ASSY. 21

CATHEDRAL OF METZ 25

THE SYNAGOGUE OF THE HADASSAH-HEBREW
  UNIVERSITY MEDICAL CENTER 65

UNION CHURCH OF POCANTICO HILLS 97

UNITED NATIONS SECRETARIAT BUILDING 117

TUDELEY CHURCH 133

THE FRAUMÜNSTER, ZURICH 139

CHAGALL IN THE RHEIMS WORKSHOP 149

LIST OF ILLUSTRATIONS

"Peace" window of the U.N. Secretariat Building *(detail)* . . . . . frontispiece

NOTRE DAME DE TOUTE GRACE CHURCH, PLATEAU D'ASSY

Window of the Assy Baptistery 18

Preliminary sketch for one of the Assy Baptistery windows 19

Preliminary sketch for one of the Assy Baptistery windows 22

Window of the Assy Baptistery 23

CATHEDRAL OF METZ

Plan of the Cathedral of Metz 26

Cartoon for the second window of the north apse 33

Cartoon for the first window of the north apse 34

Cartoon for the window of the north transept, west side 35

"Moses Receives the Tables of the Law" 38

"David and Bathsheba" 39

"David and Bathsheba" *(detail)* 40

"Jeremiah and the Exodus of the Jewish People" 42

"Abraham's Offering." "Jacob Wrestling with the Angel" 44

"Jacob's Dream." "Moses Before the Burning Bush" 45

"Moses Before the Burning Bush" *(detail)* 47

"The Creation of Man" *(detail)* 49

"The Creation of Man." "The Creation of Eve" 52

"Eve and the Serpent." "Adam and Eve Driven Out of Paradise" . . 53

"Flowers." "Beast, Flowers and Bird." "Wreath of Flowers" 56, 57

"Small Bouquet" 58, 59

"Bouquet and Rainbow." "Flowers and Birds." "Wreath of Flowers" . 60-61

"Large Bouquet" 62-63

3

SYNAGOGUE OF THE HADASSAH-HEBREW UNIVERSITY MEDICAL CENTER

Plan of the Hadassah Medical Center Synagogue 66
Window of "The Tribe of Reuben" 73
Window of "The Tribe of Simeon" 75
Window of "The Tribe of Levi" 77
Window of "The Tribe of Judah" 79
Window of "The Tribe of Zebulun" 81
Window of "The Tribe of Issachar" 83
Window of "The Tribe of Dan" 85
Window of "The Tribe of Gad" 87
Window of "The Tribe of Asher" 89
Window of "The Tribe of Naphtali" 91
Window of "The Tribe of Joseph" 93
Window of "The Tribe of Benjamin" 95

UNION CHURCH OF POCANTICO HILLS

Plan of Union Church of Pocantico Hills 98
Preliminary cartoon of "The Good Samaritan" window 100
Final cartoon of "The Good Samaritan" window 105
Window of "The Good Samaritan" 106-107
Crucifixion 108
Joel 109
Elijah 110
Daniel 111
Cherubim 112
Ezekiel 113
Jeremiah 115
Isaiah 116

UNITED NATIONS SECRETARIAT BUILDING

Final cartoon of the "Peace" window 118-119
"Peace" window (detail) 122
"Peace" window (detail) 124
"Peace" window (detail) 126
Cartoon for "Peace" window 128-129
"Peace" window (detail) 128-129
"Peace" window (detail) 131

TUDELEY CHURCH

Final cartoon for the chancel window   135

THE FRAUMÜNSTER, ZURICH

Final cartoon for the Zurich windows   141
"Madonna, Child and Offering" window *(detail)*   144
"Celestial Jerusalem" window *(detail)*.   145
"Madonna, Child and Offering" window *(detail)*   148

Trial pane for the window of "The Tribe of Joseph"   154
Trial pane for the window of "The Tribe of Zebulun"   155

All the windows illustrated in this book were made by Marc Chagall in collaboration with Charles Marq at the Jacques Simon Workshop in Reims, with the exception of the two windows for the Plateau d'Assy Baptistery, which were made at the Bony Workshop in Paris.

INTRODUCTION

Memory is a shell that must be cracked open every day so that it can be reborn on the very first day, on the day when God said: *Let there be light.* The test of Genesis continues this way: *And there was light. And God saw the light, that it was good: and God divided the light from the darkness. And God called the light Day, and the Darkness he called Night. And the morning and the evening were the first day.* After abundant darkness, it is the light that every living creature is invited to enjoy: from black to white is a passage to eternity, to the virgin sheet or sphere which is not yet colored or on which no brush has left a mark. *All things are white in God's hand so that they might be stained* a very ancient alchemic text asserts. Is there any better way to guide man's progress amid the creation, to define the very act which allows him to assess and understand the universe, in which he is not a disconnected fragment but the complete image of the whole?

By coloring and engraving man makes the Creation visible, indicating both his identity with the cosmos and his distinctness from it. This act of coloring and engraving is inseparable from the very act of being conscious. Therefore, what better symbol is there than the stained-glass window if one wants to get as close as possible to the human work as it expands according to the decree of the Revelation? Does not the very glass, this mixture of sand and ash that a sunbeam can cross without breaking, provide the

9

most beautiful receptacle for light? It can shelter it without imprisoning it, preserving its original purity. Thus the painter, when using this medium, is nearer the fountainhead than when he tackles a wall or a canvas. He is invited to enjoy the white light of the Creation. He is called upon to make visible by means of color the things that are bathed in the unadulterated light of the first day, thus revealing himself and emulating the Creator.

And since I am at the dawn of the world, I cannot help hearing the crowing of the rooster successively in Jerusalem, Zurich, Metz, Assy, Tudeley, New York and Pocantico Hills, when the first beams of the very same sun spread upon Chagall's stained-glass windows over one-fourth of the world. At this point, I must by-pass the chance location of those commissions to marvel at Providence, which has allowed a painter who is most profoundly and most authentically anchored in Tradition, in the Scriptures and in the Sacred, to punctuate the circumnavigation of the sun with these shadowless monuments on which the Word bursts into fire and sparkles with colored flames every morning, rises until noon and goes down at dusk, as if to lap at the milky night from which it will be reborn the next day in the same process of juvenescence.

If *the eye is listening,* we must still strain our ears in order to perceive this silence, which is changed from empty whiteness into music by means of color. And in this way I would like to make palpable to the heart the musical quality of this work of glass, to show it as a gift restored to the white light of divine wisdom, in the same way that the sonorous work of Mozart is a gift restored to the silence of God. Furthermore, I want to point out that what was absolutely obvious in Chagall's other works is strengthened in the windows by the power of evidence: I refer to his ability not to interfere with the movement of life, but on the contrary to experience its vibrations without hindering or halting it. So far as I am concerned, I would focus my attention on what, in Chagall's windows, is given in addition to the gift, as a reward for what was not asked for, and because it was not asked for. Truly enough, the very tribulations of his life were preparing him to illuminate the great book of the Western tradition. His childhood in Vitebsk was imbued with Hassidic spirituality, which, through its spontaneous and popular mysticism, regenerates the abstruse world of the Cabbala, lets the man whose heart has been touched by God get the better of the keepers of the Law, the learned and the erudite, reaching over to the tradition of biblical prophesying. Enthusiasm is the foremost virtue; the belief held by the simple man, far from being laughed at, is an object of reverence, all the more so as it brings joy, this pantheistic joy which bears witness that God *suffuses all things and penetrates all*. But let Chagall himself call forth that legendary time, that time of the heart, with which he will never cease being in touch through every single one of his most intimate fibres:

My father, holding up his glass, told me to go and open the door.

Why open the outer door at such a late hour? To let the prophet Elijah in?

A cluster of white stars, silvery against the blue velvet background of the sky, bursts upon my eyes and my heart.

But where is Elijah and his white chariot? Perhaps he is still lingering in the front yard and, in the disguise of a puny old man, of a hunched beggar, a bag on his back and a stick in his hand, is going to step into the house.

"Here I am. Where is my glass of wine"?

... The day of forgiveness.

Slowly, gravely, the Jews display their sacred veils, wet with tears after a whole day of praying.

Their garments unfurl like fans. The sound of their voices penetrates into the arch whose wickets are now in view now hidden. I am gasping for air. I remain motionless.

Infinite day! Take hold of me, bring me nearer to you. Utter a word! Explain!

So it is, all day long I hear "Amen!" "Amen!" and I see them all kneeling.

If you do exist, make me into a blue, lunar, fiery spirit, hide me within the Torah, do something, God, for our sake, and mine!

Our spirit evaporates and, from beneath the colored windows, arms are groping upward.

Outside the dried out branches of the tall poplars sway peacefully.

In the broad daylight, small clouds swirl, vanish, melt away. The road itself is praying. The houses are crying. The sky flows on all sides.

My memory is on fire.

And in our mind, almost compulsively, this fire is echoed by the fever of the man who was one of Chagall's first friends in France, I mean Cendrars, the poet who wrote *Easter in New York:*

Where are the long services and where the beautiful canticles?
Where are the liturgies and the music?

Where are your proud prelates, Lord, and where your nunneries?
Where the white dawn, sweet to holy men and women?

Paradise's beatitude is drowned in dust,
The mystical fires glitter no more in the stained-glass windows.

. . .

Lord, I am all alone and feverish...
My bed is cold like a coffin...

Lord, I close my eyes and my teeth chatter...
I am too lonely. I am cold. I call you...

A hundred thousand tops are whirling before my eyes...
No, a hundred thousand women... No, a hundred thousand cellos...

I think, Lord, of my unhappy hours...
I think, Lord, of my vanished hours...

I no longer think of You. I no longer think of You.

Through Cendrars, Chagall made the acquaintance of Vollard, who asked him in 1930 to illustrate the Bible. In 1931 he took his first trip to Palestine; in 1939, his pilgrimage to Rembrandt's works. The Bible etchings were not to be published until 1959, after the completion of the first pieces for the *Biblical Message* and his first stained-glass windows.

Far from enticing him away from the emotions of his childhood, his adult life strengthened him in the star-like trajectory that he recorded in his work, varied by the use of different media and techniques but never ruptured by the temptation to conform to the demands of fashion. He did not care to be modernistic; it was enough for him to trust in the vital and perpetual movement in which revelation and resurrection are continually being renewed. He is too deeply immersed in the sense of mystery, the sense of the unknowable, to attempt to translate it into logical terms: the heir to the two Testaments, his major concern is never to let will power and rationalism interfere with this fresh ignorance which enables him to know that every work of art is a manifestation of the inner light and that

> *Only mine*
> *Is the land within my soul.*

Rembrandt can only have confirmed him in this act of faith. His travels to the Near East can only have enlightened and strengthened the path he had followed for so many years. Thus the man who has been visited does not reckon the number of his days but on each and every day glorifies the flame which he feeds with his own self. And this reminds me of El Greco, who also came from the East and who made manifest in Toledo a Byzantium that had remained invisible for so long. In the same way, Chagall, through the magic of blood and immemorial nuptial feasts, in an absolutely novel and unexpected efflorescence, becomes the time and place of the many different saps that caused the wood of icons and the tree of Jesse on ancient windows to grow.

His holy land, Canaan, is the country of his soul. He is certainly not indifferent to the fact that Egypt, Greece, Palestine have been the cradles of the message: geography and history pervade the myth with the colors that the painter and the poet will use to make it perceptible. But childhood, but home, but the love dedicated to father, to mother, to a woman, all these remain for Chagall the holy land, Canaan, the country of the soul. Is this an approach to the secret of the painter's cherished chemistry? Organic chemistry and spiritual chemistry are here inseparable, just as colors and dyes are inseparable, just as a bird and his song are one. Music's mutability. What vanishes with the flow of time, what the heart and the memory attempt to preserve, that was what light was trusted to convey. With the staining of glass, it was light alone that one strove to hold back for an instant, like a unicorn. Musically inhabited, inhabiting the innermost land of the sacrament, Chagall was to find in the stained-glass window a perfectly adequate dwelling, a foot-loose dwelling that a single bush could cover with blossoms, in which the flower, the bough, the wing, tears, stars, fire, feelings, emotions, prayers, rejoicing and suffering would all be part of the same nature that we can rightly call musical.

When Chagall was introduced to the space of the stained-glass window, he was given the privilege of being more transparent, more weightless because of the very gravity of the song. He was being chosen; himself did not choose. His subject matter had been his whole life, since early childhood. To borrow an image dear to Cendrars, the poet closest to Chagall's heart, the window of the temple was to become the necessary membrane for osmosis between the heart of man and the heart of the world. What did the undertaking demand? That he illuminate the Book that had illuminated him. A humble task, as well as an immeasurable one, in which humility alone would be powerful enough for him to be received in the anonymous communion of the Chartres and the Bourges craftsmen. This Chagall had been aware of even before he started, had always been aware of it. And he is seized with enthusiasm because he clearly realizes that this is an opportunity for him to offer sincere thanks for the gift he has received. The artist frees himself, just as he knows he is made free, by a compact which vindicates what centuries and millennia have proclaimed, namely that the work of art, long ignored as such, never grows or expands if it is not grounded in the spiritual.

What Chagall also knows is that the stained-glass window is ruled by a destiny entirely different from that of the painting: first on account of the place, which is neither the collector's gallery nor the museum. Also on account of the eyes that will look at it, which are not amateurs' but worshippers' eyes. He will let others discuss techniques; his job is to impart the urge to pray to the onlookers, the eye giving precedence to the heart as a mode of perception. What Chagall wishes is that his work should be assimilated by the architecture of the place as well as by those gathered by the same faith. He wants not to impose his imprint but to mingle his own music with the song that everyone secretly whispers. And when his window is seen inserted in the stone for which it was destined, our first emotion is born from that sudden evidence that Chagall has exalted his gifts only to give them away. And in this submission he reveals to us and makes us see what the blinkers of custom had gradually obscured. For it is true that Chagall is a man who awakens. His vision cannot flourish in lethargy. Ceaselessly nourished by his sensibility and his feelings, it animates the whole space where it takes shape and vibrates into the hearts of his fellow creatures. And it is clear that it is not out of carelessness or indifference that he by-passed fashion but out of an irresistible necessity, a compulsion to obey the commands of his blood, the deep music whose perception he was blessed to find within himself.

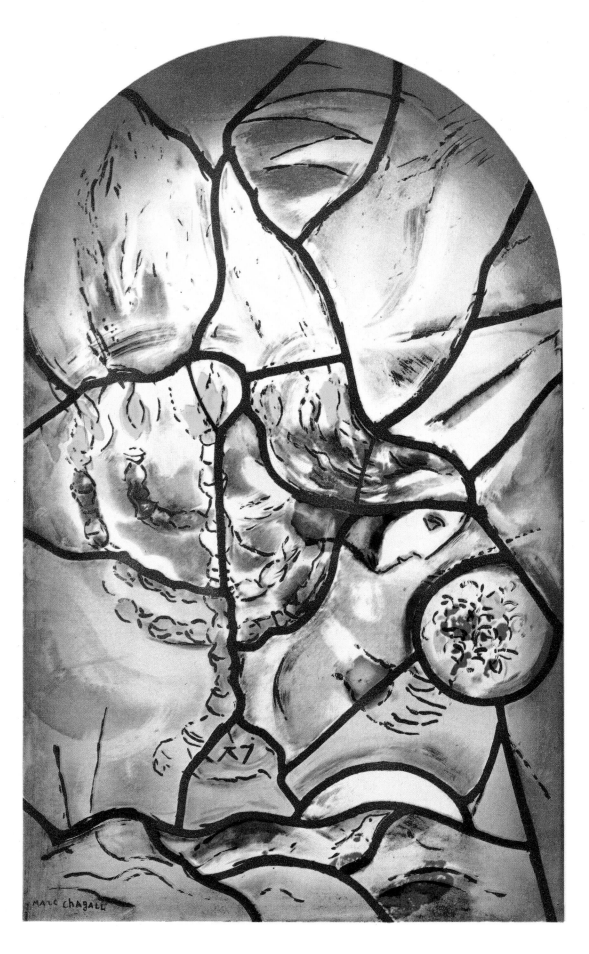

Window of the Assy Baptistery. 1957.

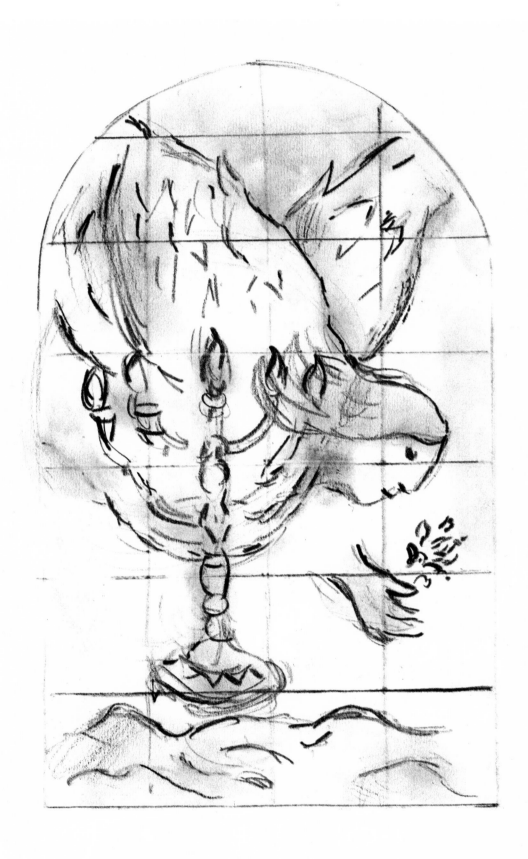

Preparatory drawing for one of the Assy Baptistery windows.

In this way his whole work acquires a particularly clear meaning in his windows: it seems to me that all the intuitive experience of Chagall is there brought into focus, that in them are fused together the finding and the spelling out of tradition and intuition. Not having to bother with invention and its undercurrent of cerebral activity, he discovers in his net of images the living verve that permanence constantly needs in order to perpetuate itself, whose truth is called life and movement. The discoveries of the heart, that is what Chagall offers us, and such is the offering that he provides between earth and heaven for the sun to diffuse its beams.

Need we add that Chagall has the great merit of having relied on the most secure traditions of the craft without renouncing a whit of his freedom and personal vision? From the outset he recognizes the art of the stained-glass window as autonomous. With him it is not a matter of transposing painting to the medium of painted glass, but a meditation at work within a specific medium. What we find here and there simultaneously are the gestures, the emotions and the unalterable unity of his nature. Not unlike the old masters, Chagall knows that the subject matter of the stained-glass window fundamentally lies in the interplay of the glass and the light. But, like them, he also knows that it is necessary to do extra teaching and moving, so as to go beyond mere virtuosity for virtuosity's sake and beyond the risk of shutting oneself off in decorative sterility. Accordingly, it seems to me natural at this point to pay homage to those who served this design when transcribing the incantation that Chagall ceaselessly renews at its fountainhead. I have in mind Brigitte and Charles Marq. The inheritors of the finest tradition, they translate into action their sensibility, their science and their technique in their workshop at Rheims. They set about their task with the gravity required by passion. They are the attentive curators of song, around which they know how to weave a lattice-work which will heighten it, rather than imprison it.

The two windows placed in the baptistery of the church of the Plateau d'Assy are born out of the white glass where some flickers of red and blue still burn occasionally while the silvery yellow under-lines the general grayness. Two angels combine their trajectories so that the fire of the Spirit may be united with the water of grace. It is an image of baptism, the perpetual act of life, which is death and resurrection. On one side the holy vase holding the primary and regenerating waters; on the other, the candlestick with six branches equally distributed right and left. *Three bowls made like unto almonds; with a knop and a flower in one branch; and three bowls made like almonds in the other branch, with a knop and a flower; so in the six branches that come out of the candlestick. And in the candlestick shall be four bowls made like unto almonds, with their knops and their flowers... And thou shalt make the seven lamps...* (Exodus XXV, 33-37.)

Chagall does not illustrate, does not describe, he only suggests. But what? Well, this impenetrable mystery in which we are steeped and which constitutes us. Look at the sphere which blooms here in the hands of the celestial messenger, it is our earth undoubtedly, and each flame around the sun is certainly a planet poised in the sky,

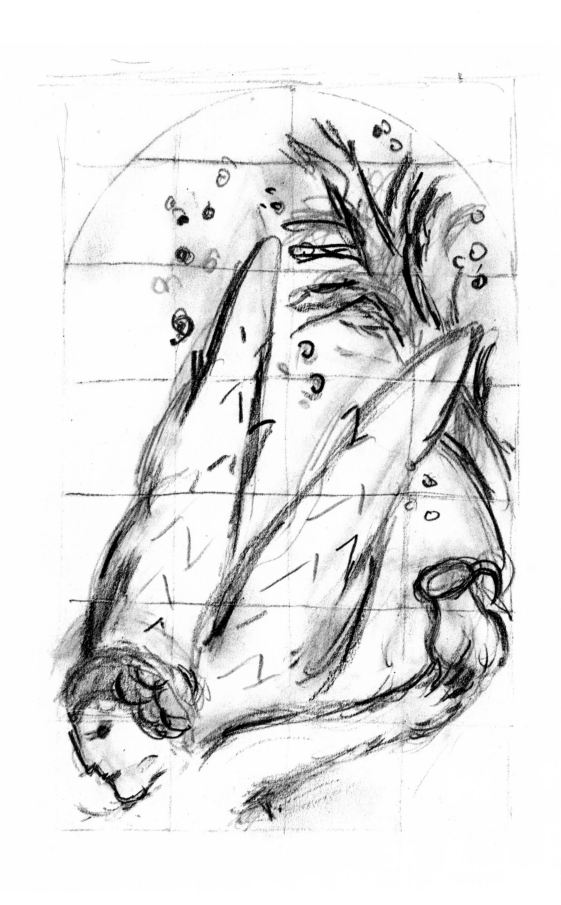

Preparatory drawing for one of the Assy Baptistery windows.

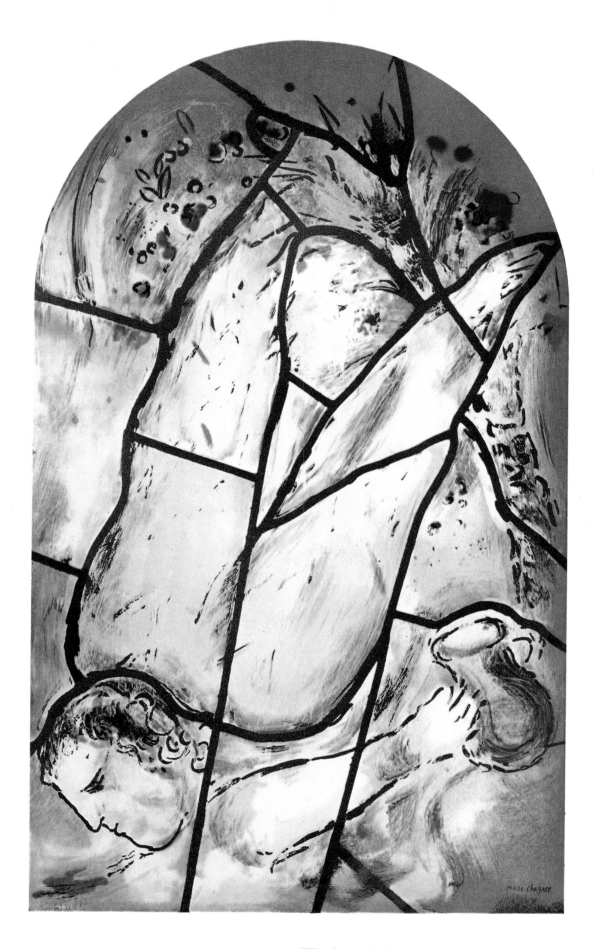

Window of the Assy Baptistery. 1957.

and, furthermore, the luminaries shedding light on the twenty-two revealed letters, the twenty-two living letters, are at once the mothers and the daughters of John's Word:

All things were made by him ; and without him was not any thing made that was made. In him was life ; and the life was the light of men. And the light shineth in darkness ; and the darkness comprehended it not. (John I, 3-5.)

It is also the dove:

I saw the Spirit descending from heaven like a dove, and it abode upon him. And I knew him not: but he that sent me to baptize with water, the same said unto me, Upon whom thou shalt see the Spirit descending, and remaining on him, the same is he which baptizeth with the Holy Ghost. (John I, 32-33.)

It is also the darkness changed into light and, at Cana, the water changed into wine:

the governor of the feast called the bridegroom, and saith unto him, Everyman at the beginning doth set forth good wine ; and when men have well drunk, then that which is worse: but thou hast kept the good wine until now. (John II, 9-10.)

The two windows are a hymn to the light that will never be overcome by darkness, to the knowledge that the carnal creature receives through the Spirit.

CATHEDRAL OF METZ

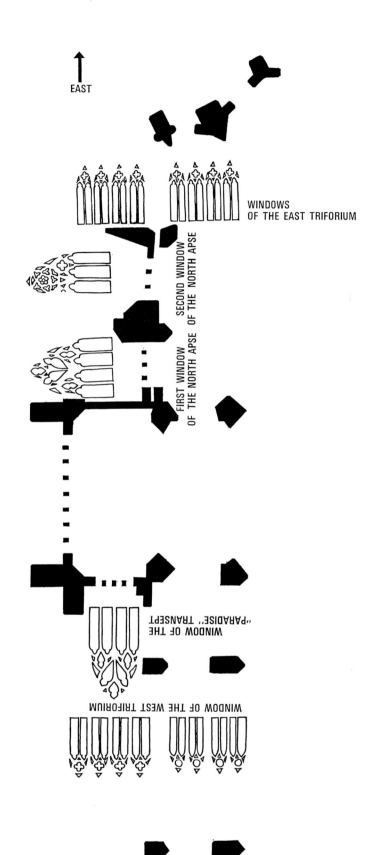

EAST

WINDOWS
OF THE EAST TRIFORIUM

SECOND WINDOW
OF THE NORTH APSE

FIRST WINDOW
OF THE NORTH APSE

WINDOW OF THE
"PARADISE" TRANSEPT

WINDOW OF THE WEST TRIFORIUM

PLAN OF THE CATHEDRAL OF METZ

SECOND WINDOW OF THE NORTH APSE

First lancet : "Moses Receives the Tables of the Law." 1959.
3.62×1.01 m. Signed bottom left : *Chagall.*

Second lancet : "David and Bathsheba." 1960.
3.62×1.01 m. Signed bottom left : *Chagall.*

Third lancet : "Jeremiah and the Exodus of the Jewish people." 1959.
3.64×1.01 m. Signed bottom right : *Chagall.*

Upper lights : "Angel Blowing a trumpet." 1.01×0.77 m.
"Symbolical sign." 1.00×1.01 m.
"Christ Surrounded by Symbols." Rose-window of 11 panels ; diameter :
2.05 m.

FIRST WINDOW OF THE NORTH APSE

First lancet : "Abraham's Offering." 1962.
3.62×0.92 m. Signed bottom left : *Chagall Reims.*

Second lancet : "Jacob Wrestling with the Angel." 1962.
3.62×0.92 m. Signed bottom right : *Chagall Reims.*

Third lancet : "Jacob's Dream." 1962.
3.62×0.92 m. Signed bottom right : *Chagall.*

Forth lancet : "Moses Before the Burning Bush." 1962.
3.62×0.92 m. Signed bottom right : *Marc Chagall.*

Upper lights : "Joseph as a shepherd." 1.41×0.88 m.
"Jacob weeps over Joseph's coat." 1.41×0.855 m.
"Noah's Ark." Right side, 2.44×0.97 m. Left side, 2.42×0.955 m.
"The Rainbow as Token of the Covenant." 1.387×0.835 m.
"The Bird." 1.26×0.395 m.
"The painter's hand." 1.295×1.235 m.

THE WINDOW OF THE NORTH TRANSEPT, WEST SIDE

First lancet : "The Creation of Man." 1963.
3.55×0.90 m. Signed bottom left : *Chagall Reims 1963.*

Second lancet : "The Creation of Eve." 1963.
3.55×0.90 m. Unsigned.

Third lancet : "Eve and the Serpent." 1964.
3.55×0.90 m. Unsigned.

Fourth lancet : "Adam and Eve Driven Out of Paradise." 1964.
3.55×0.90 m. Unsigned.

Upper lights : "Flowers and Animals." 1.385×0.77 m.
"Flowers and Animals." 1.405×0.765 m.
"Figures." 1.33×0.76 m.
"Asher and Moses." Left side, 2.36×0.855 m. Right side, 2.31×0.84 m.
"Lion." 1.27×0.44 m.
"Fish." 1.265×0.76 m.

From 1958 to 1968 Chagall works for the Cathedral of Metz. He illuminates three windows and the triforium, setting his most extensive poem into the gothic stone.

The more our time refuses to see the whole face of the world and restricts its gaze to a very small fragment of its skin, the more anguished I grow when considering this face in its eternal rhythms and the more intent I am on fighting against the general trend.

I store away the painter's words as his brush is setting the Sinai aflame. But first *there was under his feet as it were a paved work of a sapphire stone, and as it were the body of heaven in his clearness... And the Lord said unto Moses, Come up to me into the mount, and be there: and I will give thee tables of stone.* (Exodus XXIV, 10 & 12.)

That red up there, that devouring red, is the divine Love as it is perceived by the people down below. Moses alone is allowed into the mystery: sucked upward, he is a flame in the fire, a torch and a twisted fringe. He wears on his forehead the white horns of lightning, a single foot still treading the ground as his whole body is ascending the ladder that the angels are wont to climb. He receives the stone, the donum Dei that the alchemists are searching for, materializing the spirit and spiritualizing the matter. And this twofold current, the very principle of life that is symbolized by both the double beat of the heart and the death-resurrection couple, this restless stream which is the vertiginous drift of the Universe, recaptured in the lead network of the stained-glass window, suddenly burns, spreads, casts its gleam upon the crowd of the desert while a solitary witness, Aaron, already fancies himself invested with the priesthood.

David now: godlike virtues, human manifestations, the springtime of the tree of Jesse. What David, the harp-player, receives is the greenness of breath, of the wind (viento verde as Lorca would have it), of the sap, of the creation; he is Orpheus, the regulator of chaos, the poet inspired by God, who establishes order and peace through the power of music. Toward him we see Bathsheba coming, the feminine principle of the world awakened by love. To those nuptial festivities are convened the sun, the men, the animals, the entire cosmos given over to dancing and gleefulness.

Fright, cruelty, horror, the crucifixion, the bird of nightmare, the book scoffed at, the invested city,

(He cast down from heaven unto the earth the beauty of Israel)

the veiled light, the fall, the return to chaos; stains, bites, soiled colors, splotches as if left by the lees of wine;

(His children have been carried away captive before the oppressor)

Would that God had ordained that the prophesies should not be accomplished! Jeremiah, so sweet and so loving in heart, why were you chosen even before you were conceived in your mother's womb, you, the oracle of the Lord?

Why were you chosen in times when only woe could be augured? Why did you have to oppose all—kings, priests, false prophets, people of influence and the smaller fry—without being able to open the eyes of anyone, without being able to delay the slow lingering death of the kingdom of Judah?

What a contrast with the preceding window! But also what a masterful triptych is composed by those three works! See how Chagall can tremulously twang the three taut strings of his instrument, in a single stroke of his bow revealing the knowledge, in which human love is poised between the two poles of the divine revelation and of the misery subsequent to the veiling of God.

Higher up, the center of the sphere and of the rose whose petals he links together, Christ still crucified over and over, even in heaven, by the men blind to the reality of the Spirit.

Given the office of the priesthood by Melchizedek, who made offerings of bread and wine to the Almighty, Abraham stands here bathed in the blue hue diffused by the wisdom made manifest by the breath of the Creator. No sign of doubt on his face, marked only by the loftiest obedience; to Isaac his son he answered: *God will provide himself a lamb for the burnt offering*; this is

Page 33 : SECOND WINDOW OF THE NORTH APSE. Watercolor, 1.32 × 0.82 m.

"Moses Receives the Tables of the Law."
"David and Bathsheba."
"Jeremiah and the Exodus of the Jewish People."
Upper lights :
"Angel Blowing a Trumpet."
"Christ Surrounded by Symbols." Rose window of 11 panels.

Page 34 : FIRST WINDOW OF THE NORTH APSE. Watercolor, 1.43 × 0.93 m.

"Abraham's Offering."
"Jacob Wrestling with the Angel."
"Jacob's Dream."
"Moses Before the Burning Bush."
Upper lights :
"Joseph as a shepherd."
"Jacob Weeps over Joseph's Coat."
"Noah's Ark."
"The Rainbow as a token of the Covenant."
"The Bird."
"The Painter's Hand."

Page 35 : WINDOW OF THE NORTH TRANSEPT, WEST SIDE. Watercolor, 1.45 × 0.95 m.

"The Creation of Man."
"The Creation of Eve."
"Eve and the Serpent."
"Adam and Eve Driven Out of Paradise."
Upper lights :
"Flowers and Animals."
"Figures."
"Asher and Moses."
"Fish."
"Lion."

the moment when it is said (Genesis XXII, 9-10): *And they came to the place which God had told him of; and Abraham built an altar there, and laid the wood in order, and bound Isaac his son, and laid him on the altar upon the wood. And Abraham stretched forth his hand and took the knife to slay his son. And the angel of the Lord called unto him out of heaven, and said, Abraham, Abraham: and he said, here am I. And he said, Lay not thine hand upon the lad, neither do thou any thing unto him: for now I know that thou fearest God, seing thou hast not withheld thy son, thine only son from me.*

This, a premonition of crucifixion, the supreme sacrifice, when God lets himself be the holocaust in the fire of the cross. Prefiguring Christ, Isaac enlightens us with his meek and total innocence.

Jacob has crossed over the ford. Can he see the fiery wings of his opponent? *Tell me, I pray thee, thy name. And he said, Wherefore is it that thou dost ask after my name? And he blessed him there. And Jacob called the name of the place Peniel: for I have seen God face to face, and my life is preserved.* (Genesis XXXII, 29-30.)

Jacob fought: he received unto himself divine, intemporal power, which is love and light; he sees and experiences the real nature of the world that is illustrated on the ladder by the two inverted angels, a double and similar movement of the forces that only this metaphor can make visible.

Chagall knows that the color of a flame changes according to the wood that feeds it: the bush in front of Moses is suffused with a blue tinge without endangering its tender flower-like hues; on the contrary, this fire causes the tallest blossoms to open out, this fire is the fountainhead of the green water of the saps and the streams.

Darkness has received the light and has given birth to the world, to the stars, to the sun which animates all things, the very image of Christ, ceaselessly crucified and resurrected. The everlasting Virgin is leaning above him, a chalice in which childhood is restlessly renewed. Red: divine love in action. Blue: shield of wisdom upon the face and breast of the Creator. Life pulsating in the whole cosmos. *And God said, Let us make man in our image, after our likeness.* (Genesis I, 26). *In him was life; and the life was the light of men.* (John I, 4.) Having created man, God made a gift of himself, and to live is to die and be reborn in every moment to that gift. And every morning the first rays of the sun on the first lancet of the north transept reread and repeat the first chapter of the world, as the painter has there brought emergence and sprightliness to the most peaceful serenity.

Just as it has been prefigured in the unity of the sphere and in the trunk of the tree of the world, of all eternity, the couple will exist to crown the Creation. *What is below is like what is above, so that the will of God may be accomplished* so it is said in a text by Hermes Trismegistus. Eden here is the perfect mirror that reflects an unadulterated order. In every moment the world to come is enclosed; it is made flesh in Eve, the living water, the vessel

37

First lancet of the second window of the north apse.
"Moses Receives the Tables of the Law." 1959.
3.62×1.01 m. Signed bottom left : *Chagall*.

Second lancet of the second window of the north apse.
"David and Bathsheba." 1960.
3.62×1.01 m. Signed bottom left : *Chagall*.

of the Adamic fire; herself the flesh of Adam, a land out of his land, at once mother and wife. Such is the deed that can be read in the golden light that Chagall has diffused from top to bottom in the Creation of Eve, a light in which is inserted the green of the animal and vegetable world whose species were named by Adam. Vertical like him, amidst the fruits, the flowers and the branches, Nahasch stands, the serpent issued from the earth whose memory he is, whose fire he is, that throws a flimsy glow upon the belly of the woman, the mother of the human future. If there is any allusion to sin, to evil, to destruction, I would find it in the horned monster with the tawny hue, running away down below, whereas the bird in the purple cloud signals the inexhaustible raptures of love.

Lucifer, the archangel, is dazzling in the solar and divine light; Eden gives birth to the couple that is at once carnal and spiritual. Eve walks toward the blue of nights and days, toward the forests and the meadows, toward the suffering and the joy of the earth... But I want Pasternak to be heard at this point:

> *Woman, your gait and your gaze*
> *Disturb me not for a moment.*
> *Of a throat stifled by feelings*
> *The gasping sums you up whole.*
>
> *You look like a rough copy.*
> *A verse from another cycle, or as if*
> *From my rib indeed you had been*
> *Drawn while I was sleeping.*

41

"David and Bathsheba" (detail.)

Third lancet of the second window of the north apse.
"Jeremiah and the Exodus of the Jewish People." 1959.
3.64×1.01 m. Signed bottom right : *Chagall*.

STAINED GLASS IN THE FIRST WINDOW OF THE NORTH APSE

Page 44 : First lancet :   "Abraham's Offering." 1962.
3.62 × 0.92 m. Signed bottom left.

Second lancet :   "Jacob Wrestling with the Angel." 1962.
3.62 × 0.92 m. Signed bottom right.

Page 45 : Third lancet :   "Jacob's Dream." 1962.
3.62 × 0.92. Signed bottom right.

Fourth lancet :   " Moses Before the Burning Bush." 1962.
3.62 × 0.92 m. Signed bottom right.

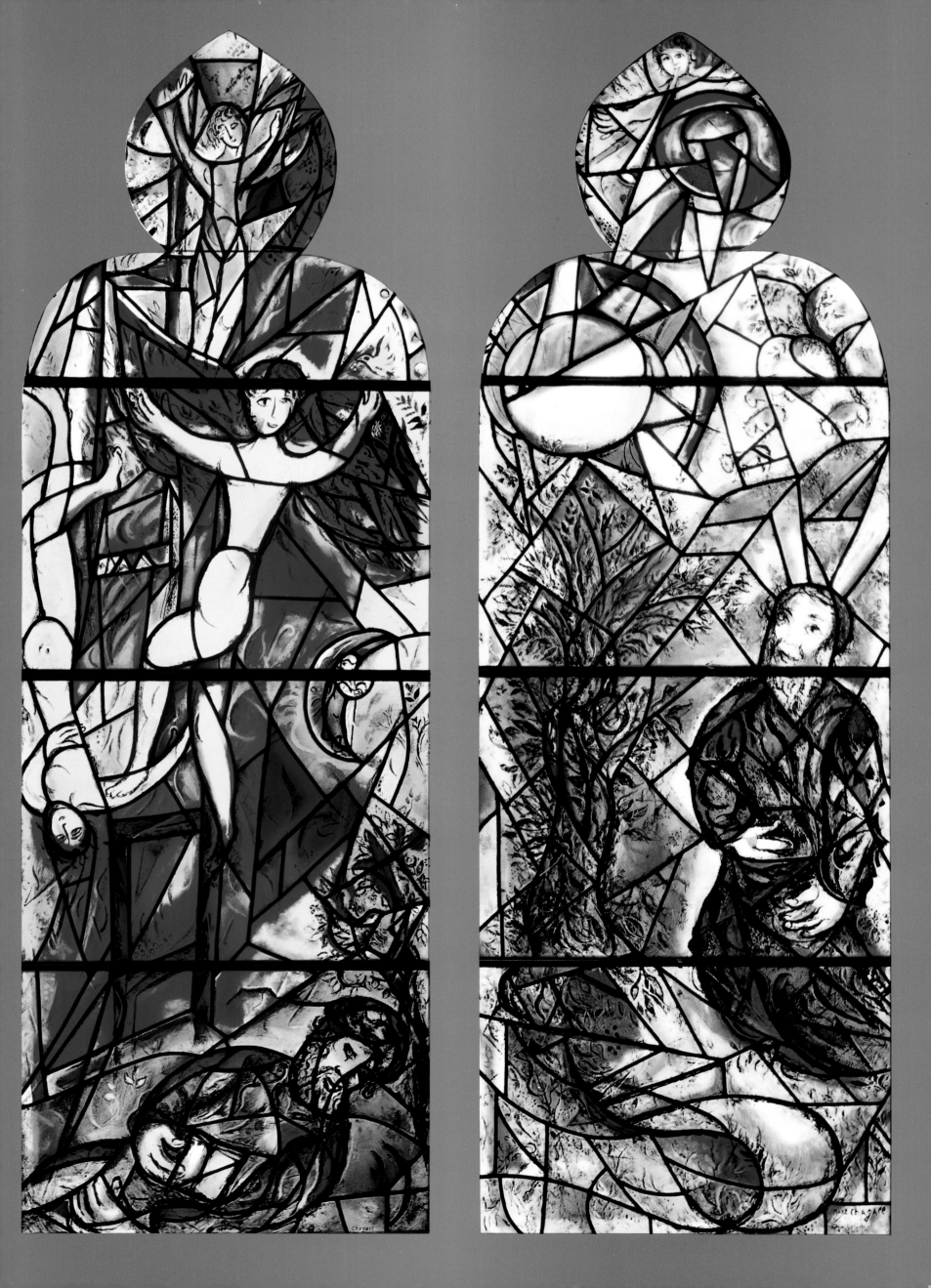

Away from my fingers at once
You slipped and nested in my palms,
Turmoil yourself and fright yourself,
A tightening in a man's heart.

(EVE)

In space, in time, in the bosom of nature, the couple is going to perpetuate the incarnation. It had been granted the power to choose. It had been destined to carry the Word, to cause the seed of eternity to germinate and fructify.

The earth is given over to the couple. Out of Eden, it set foot on the sphere that Eluard has seen as *blue like an orange.* How can this gift have been damned by the giver? Does not the love binding man to the woman spring from the fountainhead of all love, God? And is it not drawn to that fountain? Chagall stands outside the notion of curse, even outside any dualism and, beholding nature, he cannot see it as the treacherous and poisoned deed of an evil demiurge, but only as an image of divine beauty. His own gift was received as a bright mote from the single sphere, and his reaction as a painter is that of a man bringing his offering. Nature for Chagall is a reflexion of God in the curved mirror of the universe. Where could the painter look for another model? Where would his eyes rest if they were diverted from this inexhaustible splendor, ceaselessly new and never duplicated, and never discrepant or distorted, so profusely lavished upon him by the Creator? Nature for Chagall is not a mass of unknown quantities to be solved in a sum, it is the visible mystery, the light made flesh, the food of the

46

"Moses before the burning bush" (detail.) ⟫⟶

body and of the spirit. It is therefore understandable that Chagall approaches it through a hymn or a prayer. He sings it, he praises it. What it offers to his heart, his eyes, his soul and his body, he offers in return to his neighbor. It is one and the same uninterrupted process. In the same way the Greek poet would never boast of being the maker of his own song, and preferred to attribute to the divine messengers, the Muses, what his own breath had shaped within himself. Romanesque as well as gothic art gathered in the stone the labours and the days, the animals, the plants, together with the stars and the men. Similarly, Chagall continues to celebrate the nuptial feasts: within himself he urges the rhythmic power to take shape and to reach completion. He never breaks, but conversely renews the covenant so that everyone might see, under the various guise, the single source, the single purpose and the seamless robe. Is not praise of the work, praise of the worker? In his Creation, the Creator is revealed, which means that he is both hidden and visible in it. What is man in nature? The only creature that received the gift of language, or knowledge, the only one that simultaneously has the power to reap and read and, as in the days in the garden of Eden, to call, each day, *every beast of the earth and every fowl in the air and every plant produced by the earth.* It is against this background that I remember Hölderlin's words: *Man poetically dwells upon the earth.* The painter and the poet have the mission among other men to be the living examples of poetry. It is only because he is himself enlightened that man can, thanks to the sun he carries within himself, read the vast book in which he was born. His progress takes him alternately from the book of nature to the books that are written,

48

"The Creation of Man" (detail.) ⇛→

and back again. In this process his intelligence increases like a plant growing into a flower and into a fruit, like a star rising in the sky. The night steeps him in the infinite swarming of the galaxies, and every morning unveils for him the new earth where he is called to perpetuate himself, the nights and the days providing him with the visible signs in which invisibility is mirrored. Inserted in the twenty-five lancet windows of the triforium, this mirror is held up for us by Chagall after he captured in his water, or his orient, the feather and the scale, the star, the corolla, the branch, the petal, the seeds and the fruits, the wind grazing the outskirts, a gust floundering in the boughs, seasons, wings, and suns upon the sky, on the river and on the meadow; twigs in the underbrush, bird tracks, wakes left by fish; a woodcutter without his axe, he makes bundles of branches; a gardener without his pruning knife, he nevertheless brings home efflorescence and fragrance; seeing out of sheer enthusiasm, he makes visible the simple beauty that is hidden from general view by an insignificant veil. Here, the *small bouquet*, a comet, pushed along by its tail, that journeys through the sky at the end of summer, travels through the heart, touching its membrane, enlarging it, embalming it. There, a galaxy swirling away toward the boundaries of the universe: the *large bouquet* the exhilaration of spring changed into a vegetal torrent; growing, breathing; everything is born transparent so that it can acquire shape and color; curves, whirls, impetuosity, madness tamed by restraint; also a weightless dance that can awaken the vegetative soul and lead it to a spiritual awakening.

STAINED GLASS IN THE WINDOW OF THE NORTH TRANSEPT, WEST SIDE

Page 52 : *First lancet :* "The Creation of Man." 1963.
3.55 × 0.90 m. Signed bottom left.

Second lancet : "The Creation of Eve." 1963.
3.55 × 0.90 m. Unsigned.

Page 53 : *Third lancet :* "Eve and the Serpent." 1964.
3.55 × 0.90 m. Unsigned.

Fourth lancet : "Adam and Eve Driven Out of Paradise."
3.55 × 0.90 m. Unsigned.

WINDOWS OF THE TRIFORIUM OF THE NORTH TRANSEPT 1968

East side : a series of eight windows distributed along the two aisles of the transept
arm.

FIRST WINDOW :   "Beast, flowers and birds." One lancet, 3.48×0.45 m.

SECOND WINDOW :   "Flowers." Two lancets, 3.52×0.48 m.

THIRD WINDOW :   "Flowers." Two lancets, 3.51×0.48 m.

FOURTH WINDOW :   "Wreath of Flowers." Two lancets, 3.51×0.48 m.

FIFTH WINDOW :   "Wreath of Flowers." Two lancets, 3.51×0.48 m.

SIXTH WINDOW :   "Small Bouquet I." Two lancets, 3.88×0.48 m.

SEVENTH WINDOW :   "Small Bouquet II." Two lancets, 3.88×0.48 m.

EIGHTH WINDOW :   "Small Bouquet III." Two lancets, 3.90×0.48 m.

West side : a series of eight windows distributed along the two aisles of the transept
arm.

FIRST WINDOW :   "Flowers and Birds." One lancet, 3.50×0.50 m.

SECOND WINDOW :   "Wreath of Flowers." Two lancets, 3.56×0.49 m.

THIRD WINDOW :   "Bouquet and Rainbow." Two lancets, 3.58×0.50 m.

FOURTH WINDOW :   "Flowers and Birds." Two lancets, 3.48×0.50 m.

FIFTH WINDOW :   "Large Bouquet I." Two lancets, 3.59×0.49 m.

SIXTH WINDOW :   "Large Bouquet II." Two lancets, 3.48×0.49 m.

SEVENTH WINDOW :   "Large Bouquet III." Two lancets, 3.60×0.48 m.

EIGHTH WINDOW :   "Large Bouquet IV." Two lancets, 3.58×0.48 m.

Signed on the bottom of the left lancet : *Chagall Reims 1968.*

Windows of the triforium
of the north transept, east side:
Flowers.
Beasts, Flowers and Birds.
Wreath of Flowers.

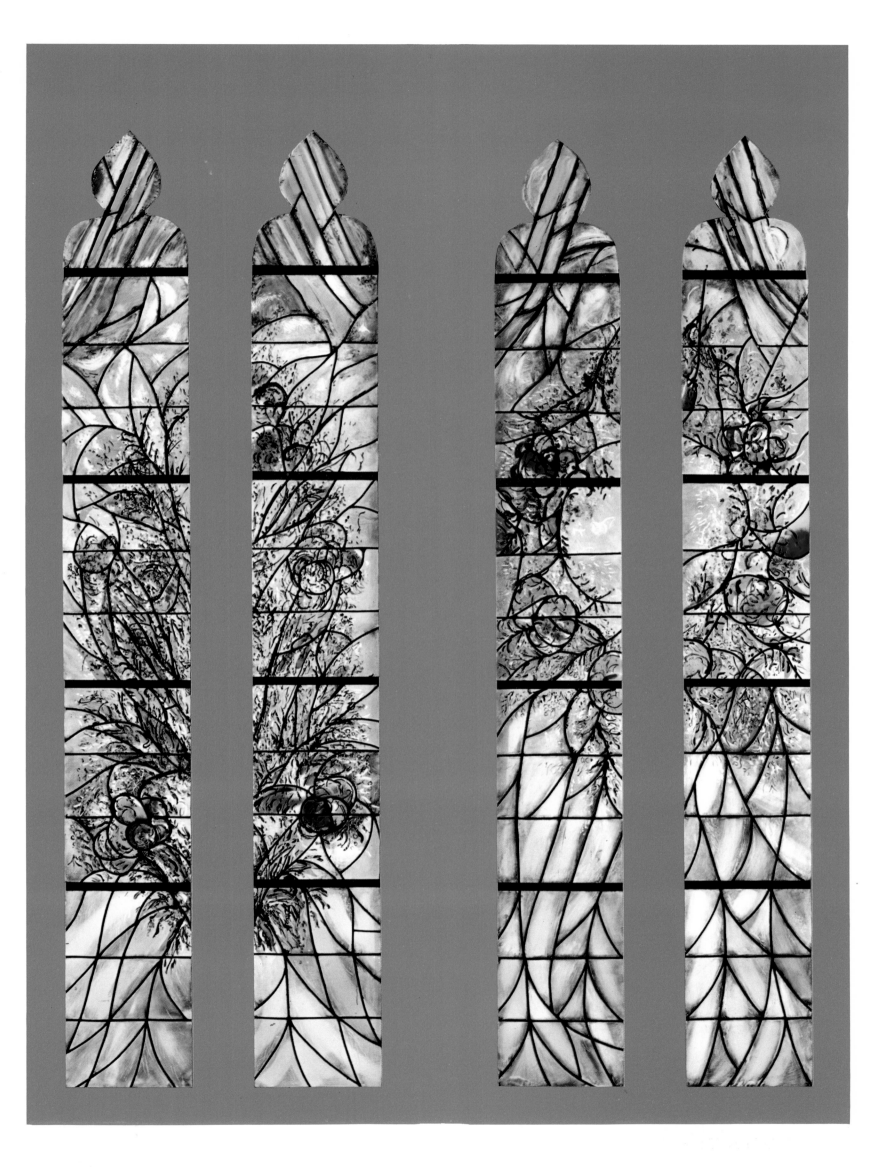

Windows of the triforium of the north transept, east side : "SMALL BOUQUET."

Windows of the triforium of the north transept, west side :

Bouquet and Rainbow.
Flowers and Birds.
Wreath of Flowers.

**Windows of the triforium
of the north transept, west side :
"LARGE BOUQUET."**

THE SYNAGOGUE
OF THE HADASSAH-HEBREW
UNIVERSITY MEDICAL CENTER

←—◄◄ "Eve and the Serpent" *(detail)*.

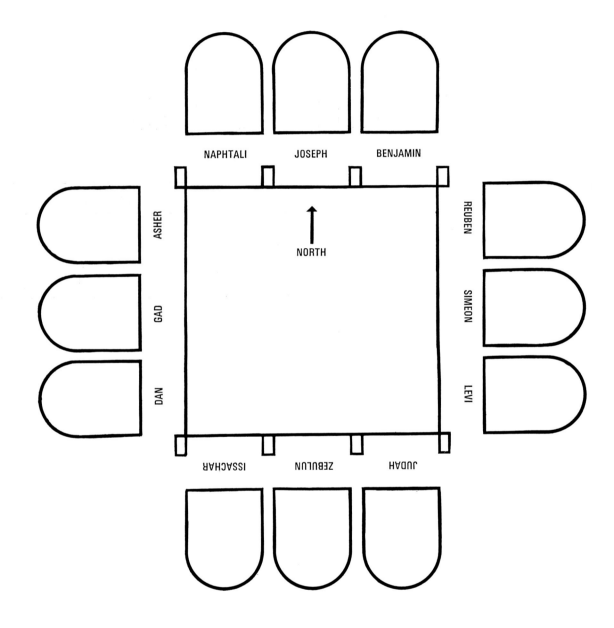

PLAN OF THE HADASSAH MEDICAL CENTER SYNAGOGUE

A series of 12 windows oriented in groups of three on the four cardinal points; all the same size, 3.38 × 2.51 m.

East side:	FIRST WINDOW :	"The Tribe of Reuben." Signed bottom right : *Chagall.*
	SECOND WINDOW :	"The Tribe of Simeon." Signed bottom right : *Chagall.*
	THIRD WINDOW :	"The Tribe of Levi." Signed bottom right : *Marc Chagall.*
South side:	FOURTH WINDOW :	"The Tribe of Judah." Engraved and signed bottom right : *Marc Chagall,* in Hebrew letters.
	FIFTH WINDOW :	"The Tribe of Zebulon." Engraved and signed bottom right : *Marc Chagall.*
	SIXTH WINDOW :	"The Tribe of Issachar." Signed bottom right : *Chagall.*
West side:	SEVENTH WINDOW :	"The Tribe of Dan." Signed bottom right : *Chagall.*
	EIGHTH WINDOW :	"The Tribe of Gad." Signed bottom right : *Marc Chagall.*
	NINTH WINDOW :	"The Tribe of Asher." Signed bottom right : *Marc Chagall Reims.*
North side:	TENTH WINDOW :	"The Tribe of Naphtali." Signed bottom right : *Chagall Reims 1961.*
	ELEVENTH WINDOW :	"The Tribe of Joseph." Signed bottom right : *Chagall 1961.*
	TWELFTH WINDOW :	"The Tribe of Benjamin." Signed bottom right : *Marc Chagall.*

When I made my etchings for the Bible I went to Israel where I found both the light and the earth, that is the substance. At Metz, for my first windows, there was stone to cope with. In Jerusalem everything is new, but here I have my talisman. When you are twenty you don't bother about substance. To do so you must have gone through suffering, or have grown old. Sometimes I am told: "But, Chagall, you are unsubstantial," and I answer: "You have to be unsubstantial to understand what substance has to say."

So Chagall speaks, and he goes on, still referring to the windows destined for the synagogue of the Hadassah Medical Center: *When they are assembled, they will form a kind of crown. Each color must be an enticement to pray...* adding: *I cannot pray myself, I can only work.*

It is said (Numbers IX, 15-16): *And on the day that the tabernacle was reared up, the cloud covered the tabernacle, namely, the tent of the testimony; and at even there was upon the tabernacle as it were the appearance of fire, until the morning. So it was always; the cloud covered by day and the appearance of fire by night.* The tabernacle, which is the tent of the testimony, is now the synagogue, and the cloud that crowns it with the appearance of fire is the celestial ring or the migrating sun. The celestial crown is, in effect, the twelve glass houses that Chagall built beneath the Judean sky, so that the sun could pull them each morning from the night, visit them each day, and bless them with its rays, a daily reminder of the gesture of Jacob, the father of the twelve tribes through his sons Reuben, Simeon and Levi, Judah, Zebulun, Issachar, Dan, Gad, Asher, Naphtali, Joseph, Benjamin, whom he blessed before going to join his fathers *in the cave that is in the field of Ephron the Hittite. In the cave that is before Mamre in the land of Canaan... (There they burried Abraham and Sarah his wife; there they buried Isaac and Rebekah...)* (Genesis XLIX, 29-31.)

This is a reminder that the synagogue, like all temples, is an earthly reflection of the cosmos, and the tabernacle is a reflection of the Lord, just as every man is himself a microcosm and a temple where God dwells in the form of the source of light. Just as the sky was divided into twelve parts by the zodiac, so the land of Canaan, a truly celestial land as much as the other, was divided among the twelve tribes. It is the act of the universe that Chagall brings back to us by coloring the twelve units of glass, by coloring the white light of Judea, by working with red, blue, yellow, green, by drawing and by using black as a filter. It is a lattice-work, a locked cage that imprisons neither the wing nor the song, a cage to extoll effusion, to make the visible transparent, to color the wave and the vibration, a cage whose squirrel is the sun of the nativity, Jacob, who gives birth and who gives names.

REUBEN

Reuben thou art my firstborn,
my might and the beginning of my strength,
the excellence of dignity and the excellence of power:
Unstable as water, thou shalt not excel;

(Genesis XLIX, 3-4.)

Sapphire predominates in this window, "the fairest thing," which Moses' rod was said to have been made of. Touched by the first ray, it changes from indigo blue to azure blue; every morning in its midst the primordial waters teeming with gems, sea-weed and fish are brought to life after being impregnated by the winged fire. In this house life starts anew with each dawn. In this place each dawn is the first one happening in the world. Its vigor is not blunted. Impetus, perpetual renewal, this is what is meant by the drawing, the rhythm, the colors and the emblems.

SIMEON

Instruments of cruelty are in their habitations.

. . .

In their anger they slew a man
and in their selfwill they digged down a wall.
Cursed be their anger, for it was fierce ;
and their wrath, for it was cruel.

(Genesis XLIX, 5-7.)

The second window of the east wall: here it is always the first morning, the origin of all things made manifest by a puff of air. The bull springs into the sky and upon the earth exalts carnal, venusian love, transmuted, however, into a fountain of poetry by the winged horse. It is a time of violence, of passion, of fertility, of childbearing. The blood of the immolated bull will be swallowed by the earth so as to let Spring break into bud.

פְּרָת יוֹסֵף בֵּן פֹּרָת עֲלֵי עָיִן בָּנוֹת צָעֲדָה עֲלֵי שׁוּר

Chagall

LEVI

Chagall is now inspired by the benediction of Moses:

They have observed thy word
and kept thy covenant.
They shall teach Jacob thy judgements,
and Israel thy law.

(Deuteronomy XXXIII, 9-10.)

The ascending sun is scattering gold over the planets, over the earth, into the glass. The last days of Spring, intimations of Summer. What was dead fades and returns to dust. What has germinated and blossomed is made stronger by the light. The twofold stream of life will be infused into the cosmos, and through the priesthood of Aaron's sons the Word will remain alive.

JUDAH

Judah is a lion's whelp ;
from the prey, my son, thou art gone up ;
he stooped down, he couched as a lion,
and as an old lion ;
who shall rouse him up?
The sceptre shall not depart from Judah,
nor a lawgiver from between his feet,
until Shiloh come ;
and unto him
shall the gathering of the people be.

(Genesis XLIX, 9-10.)

"Judah is a lion's whelp." He has climbed to the highest point of the sky. He roars and blazes. He can often be seen on the southern wall of romanesque churches, where he crouches over a sundial. We are at the noontide of the world, at its zenith, at the hour of the sacrament.

ZEBULUN

Zebulun shall dwell at the haven of the sea ;
and he shall be for an haven of ships ;
and his border shall be unto Zidon.

(Genesis XLIX, 13.)

The solar fire imparts its warmth to the earth. In the ear of the wheat light has been transmuted into substance and food. It is the time of harvesting, of the first gathering of crops. On the sea purified by the summer sunbeams, immune from the dangers of tempests, the ships are sailing, burdened with all the things that the earth and the waters have yielded to man. Abundance of life: in the bottomless reserves of the sea, fish are moving; abundance of crops: already, the ritual offering that the fire will consume is being set apart.

ISSACHAR

Issachar is a strong ass
couching down between two burdens.
And he saw that rest was good,
and the land that it was pleasant.

(Genesis XLIX, 14-15.)

The labors have been completed. After the painful work in the fields, here comes the time of rest amidst the plenty of fruit. Man is enthralled by the beauty of woman, which strikes him as quite new, like a fruit ripened by summer. It is the kingdom of peace and love, favorable to the maturing of intelligence. The strong ass couching down between two burdens will get up to carry the Virgin and the Son; on Palm Sunday it will trot into Jerusalem after Christ has said to two of his disciples: *Go ye into the village over against you ; in the which at your entering ye shall find a colt tied, whereon yet never man sat: loose him, and bring him hither. And if any man ask you, Why do ye loose him? thus shall ye say unto him, Because the Lord hath need of him.* (Luke XIX, 30-31.)

DAN

Dan shall judge his people,
as one of the tribes of Israel.
Dan shall be a serpent by the way,
an adder in the path.

(Genesis XLIX, 16-17.)

"Dan shall judge his people." At the top, the sword is the beam of the balance in which the acts of men are weighed righteously and according to the law. This pair of justly balanced scales is echoed by the candlestick, which retains only two branches that extend equally on either side of the central axis, the bearer of the *sol justatiae*; this axis is itself resting on the head of the old telluric serpent which distributes death or life depending on whether it is coiled up or erect.

GAD

Gad, a troop shall overcome him:
but he shall overcome at the last.

(Genesis XLIX, 19.)

At the heart of the Creation and the abundance of gifts: shouts, war, Mars the Destroyer. The red stands for the wound, for the spilt blood. Terror runs across and tears apart the green and fertile stretch of land. Here is the ambush, here is the sword, the serpent, the beast. The sharp lines of the drawing and the rhythm of the leading make the prevalence of cruelty manifest. There is no life without death, no generation without destruction, no resurrection without a descent into hell.

ASHER

Out of Asher his bread shall be fat,
and he shall yield royal dainties.

(Genesis XLIX, 20.)

Communion of heaven and earth through bread, while oil is a symbol of grace; and Moses says in his benediction:

Let Asher be blessed with children;
let him be acceptable to his brethren,
and let him dip his foot in oil.

(Deuteronomy XXXIII, 24.)

Peace prevails. The candlestick, perfectly horizontal, underlines the balance of the world. Glowing on the altar, it enlightens and guides. The eagle carries the spiritual fire; the birds, symbol of what is volatile, bear witness to the sublimation of matter.

NAPHTALI

Naphtali is a hind let loose:
he giveth goodly words.

(Genesis XLIX, 21.)

Yellow: the birth of the new sun, the coming in of the new light, like a fawn out of the dark womb of its mother. It is the time of the star, of the shepherds, of the Annunciation angels; it is the time of the Nativity.

JOSEPH

Moses said of Joseph:

Blessed of the Lord be his land,
for the precious things of heaven, for the dew,
and for the deep that coucheth beneath,
And for the precious fruits brought forth by the sun,
and for the precious things put forth by the moon,
And for the chief things of the ancient mountains,
and for the precious things of the lasting hills,
And for the precious things of the earth and the fullness thereof,
and for the good will of him that dwelt in the bush:
let the blessing come upon the head of Joseph,
and upon the top of the head of him that was separated
                                    from his brethren.
His glory is like the firstling of his bullock,
and his horns are like the horns of unicorns:
with them he shall push the people together
to the ends of the earth.
                    (Deuteronomy XXXIII, 13-17.)

Diffuse light, vaporous blues, emerging, greens and reds, everything here suggest weightlessness. The bow and the arrow, the bird, the breath molded into music, so many signs of air. By its very structure, the window carries us aloft on its waves, and the Muses inspire us.

BENJAMIN

Benjamin shall raven as a wolf:
in the morning he shall devour the prey,
and at night he shall divide the spoil.

(Genesis XLIX, 27.)

Made lighter by the engraving, the blue becomes the substance of the upper waters. The matter is spiritualized. The elements are reunited, steeping themselves in the original source, reconstructing the initial sphere, while, conversely, the creation Begins again with the materialization of the spirit.

Ceaselessly, the fish swim in the waters of life.

UNION CHURCH
OF POCANTICO HILLS

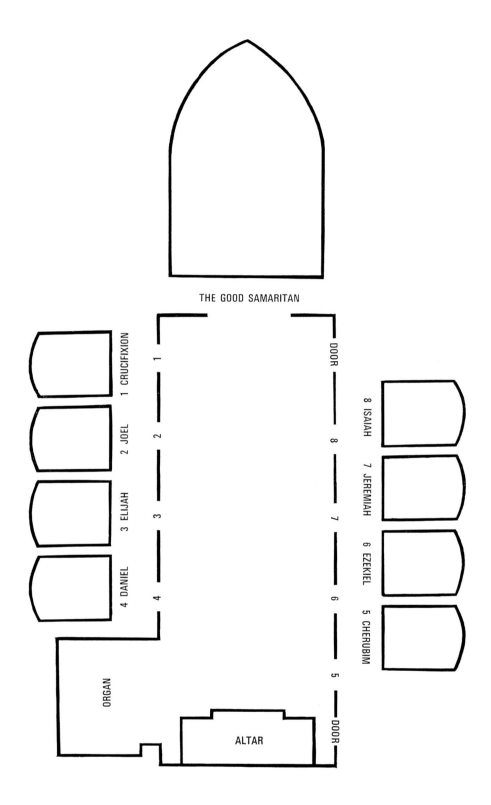

THE GOOD SAMARITAN

1 CRUCIFIXION
2 JOEL
3 ELIJAH
4 DANIEL

DOOR

8 ISAIAH
7 JEREMIAH
6 EZEKIEL
5 CHERUBIM

ORGAN

ALTAR

DOOR

PLAN OF UNION CHURCH OF POCANTICO HILLS

1964 : "The Good Samaritan," in the memory of John D. Rockefeller Jr., 4.47×2.78 m.

1966 : Series of eight windows in the chapel, all the same size : 1.48×1.18 m., dealing with the Prophets.

FIRST WINDOW :
"Crucifixion," in the memory of Michael C. Rockefeller.
Signed bottom right : *Reims Marc Chagall 1966.*

SECOND WINDOW :
"The Word of the Lord that Came to Joel."
Signed bottom left : *Marc Chagall.*

THIRD WINDOW :
"Elijah Carried Away into Heaven on a Chariot of Fire."
Signed bottom left : *Reims Marc Chagall.*

FOURTH WINDOW :
"Daniel's Vision."
Signed at bottom : *1966 Reims Marc Chagall.*

FIFTH WINDOW :
"Cherubim."
Signed bottom right : *Chagall Reims.*

SIXTH WINDOW :
"Ezekiel's Vocation."
Signed bottom right : *1966 Chagall Reims.*

SEVENTH WINDOW :
"Jeremiah's Lamentations."
Signed bottom right : *Chagall.*

EIGHTH WINDOW :
"Isaiah's Prophecy."
Signed bottom right *Reims 1966 Marc Chagall.*

Preliminary cartoon for the window of "The Good Samaritan," actual size.

THE GOOD SAMARITAN

To the dear memory of John D. Rockfeller, Jr., who died on May 11, 1960 in witness of his firm devotion to his church and to his work, this window is dedicated by his family.

And Jesus answering said, A certain man went down from Jerusalem to Jericho, and fell among thieves, which stripped him of his raiment, and wounded him, and departed, leaving him half dead. And by chance there came down a certain priest that way: and when he saw him, he passed by on the other side. And likewise a Levite, when he was at the place, came and looked on him, and passed by on the other side. But a certain Samaritan, as he journeyed, came where he was; and when he saw him, he had compassion on him, and went to him, and bound up his wounds, pouring in oil and wine, and set him on his own beast, and brought him to an inn, and took care of him. And on the morrow when he departed, he took out two pence, and gave them to the host, and said unto him, Take care of him; and whatsoever thou spendest more, when I come again I will repay thee. Which now of these three, thinkest thou, was neighbour unto him that fell among the thieves? And he said, He that shewed mercy on him. Then said Jesus unto him, Go and do thou likewise.

(Luke X, 30-37.)

On that Holy Friday of 1970 it was already Spring. For half an hour the train clattered across the huge wasteland outside New York amid automobile cemeteries, heaps of scrap-iron, bricks and discarded tires.

The Reverend Marshall L. Smith met us with his car at Tarrytown and drove us to his church in Pocantico Hills.

The Hudson river flows at the bottom of the hills. The chapel appears between the elm trees, which keep the air slightly damp and impart to the atmosphere the subtle shades that can be observed on rose petals. It is not steeped in solitude, but in a particular silence, the living silence of nature stirred by the rustling of the wind, the whirring of wings, the songs of birds. You go in: the woodwork, the stone walls and the colors do not shut you in but make you feel welcome. Nature itself is made welcome in the same way, and you experience the rare happiness of hearing in the stained-glass windows the same praise of the sunshine that is whispered by the grass and the dew, the feathers, the branches, the blackbirds and the breeze. And this praise is the prayer to which everything invites you and in which it urges you to join. It springs from a feeling of nuptials and harmony; it blooms from the inside and quivers in each petal of the window. It is uninterrupted music, a brook, a river where the world is mirrored, where the fish scales echo the spotted wing; it is a fountain for the thirsty where the poet-prophets can deeply drink. They are the witnesses of the Spirit, the oracles of God. In the wanderings, in the ruins, in the fall and the exile, they maintain the prevalence of the Light. The craftsmen of the Word, they relentlessly work, so that the crumbling walls should not engulf the Revelation. Where is the fountain from which they will draw up the water and the fire? Within themselves, for they are the transparent men of God. Through them the sun refracts its warmth and its light, stirs them up, moves them from fright to quaking. I see them shuddering as though the prophetic flux were still besieging their image. It is the greatness of Chagall to make visible by means of line and color that heaven which lives in them. Broken by history, they are reborn among the gems of the celestial City whose boundaries are measured by the angel with the golden rod. Men of visions, they are the precursors and the contemporaries of the singer of Patmos. History is not a riddle for them; it blinds the people and the princes, but it is a written book for one who keeps his eyes from the dust. In the blue, in the yellow, in the green of the windows of the Pocantico Hills chapel, time is transfigured: it is regenerated in its origin; like sunbeams it plays on the surface of water. Above and beyond the blood and the tears, what Chagall makes visible to the heart's inward eye is that flimsy and fragile plant, the prayer, a spot where colors reach the purity of that lily that Simone Martini and Leonardo da Vinci were fond of painting in their Annunciations.

In the great west window, dedicated to the memory of John D. Rockfeller, Jr., Chagall illuminates the insinuating ways of love and charity upon the earth. He knows how to fill a face with pity and sweetness, how to make a gesture carry the feelings expressed by the eyes. Everything is centered upon the Samaritan; the horse seems to be a messenger between two worlds, even as the deed of the traveller causes the angels in heaven to be joyful and alleviates the sufferings of the crucified God.

Thou shalt love thy neighbour as thyself.
— Warmth and love, Chagall rejoins, are the most important things in art.

With this window in mind, he declares:

I have introduced nothing in this work that should not be in keeping with the essence of the parable, from an inner and mystical point of view. I believe that the artist's explanation of the meaning of his work somewhat deprives it of a part of its worth. Everyone must and can understand what he himself is attempting to express, and it often turns out to be made of the same stuff as the religious emotion he experiences.

Final cartoon of the window of "The Good Samaritan." ⟫⟶

Pages 106-107 : Window of "The Good Samaritan" (detail).

CRUCIFIXION

In memory of Michael Clark Rockefeller.

Ask, and it shall be given you; seek, and ye shall find; knock, and it shall be opened unto you.

(Matthew VII, 7.)

Crucifixion on the south wall. Night grows into day, from blue to blue through crimson. Who never felt the beating of the angel's wings called the heart? Enter your own house, which is heaven unto yourself, and you will know Christ and the meaning of the Crucifixion: He will greet you on the threshold, and then you will know that the forest of Death is also the forest of Resurrection.

JOEL

And it shall come to pass afterward, that I will pour out my spirit upon all flesh; and your sons and your daughters shall prophesy, your old men shall dream dreams, your young men shall see visions: and also upon the servants and upon the handmaids in those days will I pour out my spirit. And I will shew wonders in the heavens and in the earth, blood, and fire, and pillars of smoke. The sun shall be turned into darkness, and the moon into blood, before the great and the terrible day of the Lord come.

(Joel II, 28-31.)

A vertical meadow where the grass is almost transparent. The green of the Creation. Effusion. Generated by the flesh, regenerated by the spirit. The beauty of the woman, in which the two poles of love are brought together. Joel, walking and praying: this is hope already present; this is the coming of God; this is the Pentecost.

109

ELIJAH

And it came to pass, as they still went on, and talked, that, behold, there appeared a chariot of fire, and horses of fire, and parted them both asunder; and Elijah went up by a whirlwind into heaven. And Elisha saw it, and he cried, My father, my father, the chariot of Israel, and the horsemen thereof. And he saw him no more: and he took hold of his own clothes, and rent them in two pieces.

(II Kings II, 11-12.)

Elijah reveals to his disciple the great mystery of transmutation. The perishable matter is turned into gold by the spiritual fire. Because he has seen the invisible, the disciple will receive a double portion of his master's spirit. He is now ready to walk on the path of light blazed by the chariot of knowledge that the horses of the sun drive away.

DANIEL

And it came to pass, when I, even I Daniel, had seen the vision, and sought for the meaning, then behold, there stood before me as the appearance of a man. And I heard a man's voice between the banks of Ulai, which called, and said, Gabriel, make this man to understand the vision. So he came near where I stood: and when he came, I was afraid, and fell upon my face.

(Daniel VIII, 15-17.)

Shaken by the storm of the Spirit, here is the prophet with his face toward the ground; now he gets up more alert and lively than a young willow, his face yet like a palimpsest on which words and visions are ineradicably written.

111

CHERUBIM

So he drove out the man; and he placed at the east of the garden of Eden, Cherubims, and a flaming sword, which turned every way, to keep the way of the tree of life.

(Genesis III, 24.)

Upon the Cherubim lies the throne of God. They still are the keepers of the Covenant and of the Testimony. They are part of the divine light, which the painter has translated into a serene sweetness in the ovals of their faces. They are no longer those who expel, but, on the contrary, are those who greet in the name of the Redeemer.

EZEKIEL

But thou, son of man, hear what I say unto thee ; Be not thou rebellious like that rebellious house ; open thy mouth, and eat that I give thee.

. . .

And he said unto me, Son of man, cause thy belly to eat, and fill thy bowels with this roll that I give thee.

(Ezekiel II, 8 ; III, 3.)

The sapphire stone stains the visionary prophet walking toward his own vision, as if lifted up by it. He has been elected to receive and continue the prophetic tradition: he has been chosen to receive the true food which is, allied to the twenty-two signs, the revelatory word of the universe.

113

JEREMIAH

Aleph

I am the man that hath seen affliction
by the rod of his wrath.
He hath led me, and brought me
into darkness, but not into light.
Surely against me is he turned ;
he turneth his hand against me all the day.

My flesh and my skin hath he made old ;
he hath broken my bones.
He hath builded against me,
and compassed me with gall and travail.
He hath set me in dark places,
as they that be dead of old.

He hath hedged me about, that I cannot get out:
he hath made my chain heavy.
Also when I cry and shout,
he shutteth out my prayer.
He hath inclosed my ways with hewn stone,
he hath made my paths crooked.

(Lamentations III, 1-9.)

Jeremiah! the poet-prophet that Chagall likes best. Sensitive, meek and peaceful, he constantly had to utter oracles of despair. Against him, who is full of love for his neighbour, turn the powerful as well as the poor, so blinded are they by corruption, idolatry and sensual pleasures. Repeating the prophecy in the tenderest part of his heart, Jeremiah lets his tears flow, he cries, powerless, over the destiny of his people. Here are the fall, the exile, the deportations. Here also is the whispered dialogue between the soul and her God.

115

ISAIAH

As for me, this is my covenant with them, saith the Lord ; My spirit that is upon thee, and my words which I have put in thy mouth, shall not depart out of thy mouth nor out of the mouth of thy seed, nor out of the mouth of thy seed's seed, saith the Lord, from henceforth and for ever.

(Isaiah LIX, 21.)

Reward of Yahweh's servant. The angel, messenger of the Lord, appears here to confirm the words put in the prophet's mouth. So much suffering has not been in vain if it paves the way for the new covenant and the redemption. God's poet, having abolished his own will as an obstacle in the way of the gift, receives the living and eternal word just as a flower receives the dew of the sky in its corolla.

UNITED NATIONS
SECRETARIAT BUILDING

Window dedicated to the memory of Dag Hammarskjöld and his companions, killed in duty on September 17, 1961.

Gift of Marc Chagall and the Staff of the United Nations, Dedicated on September 17, 1964.

Inner size : 3.23×4.80 m. Together with the band : 3.58×5.38 m.

It was Good Friday. The city was wrapped in mist. Walking down toward the United Nations headquarters to see the window that Chagall has devoted to the Kingdom of the Messiah, was it possible for me on that very day not to associate Chagall's name with that of the poet of "Easter in New York"?

In long strides I go downtown,
With my back hunched up, my heart wrinkled, my mind feverish.

. . .

It is at this hour, the ninth of the day,
That your Head, Lord, leaned upon your Heart.

I am sitting by the Ocean's shore...

I remember a blue gem set in the grey uniformity of that mist. I remember journeying from one blue to another blue, I remember the muted sound of the reds, the light palpitations of the yellows, the greens strewn like fragments of meadows among the flowers. It is not the blue of summer, neither is it that of the sea; it is not the red of blood; it is not the yellow of gold, nor the green of a field, but rather the tree of the world, of Eden starting anew, of the Kingdom come all wrapped up together.

Among so much misery and suffering, the one who saw the throne, the seraphim and the King, Isaiah, the one whose lips were burnt by the purifying embers, Isaiah, inspired by the Lord, is

120

able to see the Creation again in the transparency of the first morning, and

The people that walked in darkness have seen a great light:
they that dwell in the land of the shadow of death,
upon them hath the light shined.

(Isaiah IX, 2.)

This timeless instant Chagall has chosen to make visible in the poem born out of crystal. Over such a heap of ruins and woes, a star has risen. The earth has become a celestial thing. The flames of the single source, the first breath transmogrify the dry wood into a living joy. It is revealed to everyone that heaven is within him, dwelling there and inhabiting him. The shepherds, the angels, the birds announce the good news:

 Thou hast multiplied the nation,
the seer asserts,
  and not increased the joy:
  they joy before thee according to the joy in harvest,
  and as men rejoice when they divide the spoil.

(Isaiah IX, 3.)

All wealth is spread over all creatures. The cross will no longer be the tree of death but the tree of resurrection and life:

And there shall come forth a rod out of the stem of Jesse,
and a branch shall grow out of his roots.

(Isaiah XI, 1.)

121

"Peace" window of the United Nations Secretariat Building in New York. *(detail).* ⟫⟶

The Kingdom of the Messiah

Thou hast multiplied the nation,
and not increased the joy:
they joy before thee according to the joy in harvest,
and as men rejoice when they divide the spoil.
For thou hast broken the yoke of his burden,
and the staff of his shoulder,
the rod of his oppressor,
as in the day of Midian.
For every battle of the warrior is with confused noise,
and garments rolled in blood ;
but this shall be with burning
and fuel of fire.
For unto us a child is born,
unto us a son is given:
and the government shall be upon his shoulder:
and his name shall be called
Wonderful, Counsellor, The mighty God,
The everlasting Father, The Prince of Peace.
Of the increase of his government and peace,
there shall be no end,
upon the throne of David, and upon his kingdom,
to order it,
with judgement and with justice from henceforth even for ever:
the zeal of the Lord of hosts will perform this.

(Isaiah IX, 3-7.)

←〰 "Peace" window of the United Nations Secretariat Building. *(detail)*.

Rejoicing is upon the earth as it is in heaven: justice and harmony and grace regulate the perfect balance of the universe; the peace between man and God restores the original peace of nature; "like a perfect chemist," the painter turns the very humble matter into a precious stone, and the future into present: it is the kingdom of the Messiah.

And there shall come forth a rod out of the stem of Jesse,
and a branch shall grow out of its roots:
And the spirit of the Lord shall rest upon him,
the spirit of wisdom and understanding,
the spirit of wisdom and might,
the spirit of knowledge and of the fear of the Lord;
And shall made him quick of understanding in the fear of the Lord:
and he shall not judge after the sight of his eyes,
neither reprove after the hearing of his ears:
But with righteousness shall he judge the poor,
and reprove with equity for the meek of the earth:
and he shall smite the earth with the rod of his mouth,
and with the breath of his lips shall he slay the wicked.
And righteousness shall be girdle of his loins,
and faithfulness the girdle of his reins.

(Isaiah XI, 1-5.)

←〰 "Peace" window of the United Nations Secretariat Building. *(detail)*.

The wolf also shall dwell with the lamb,
and the leopard shall lie down with the kid ;
and the calf and the young lion and the fatling together
and a little child shall lead them.
And the cow and the bear shall feed ;
their young ones shall lie down together:
and the lion shall eat straw like the ox.

(Isaiah XI, 6-7.)

←▬ "Peace" window of the United Nations Secretariat Building. *(detail).*

Cartoon for the "Peace" window of the United Nations Secretariat Building *(detail)*.

"Peace" window of the United Nations Secretariat Building *(detail)*.

And the suckling child shall play on the hole of the asp,
and the weaned child shall put his hand on the cockatrice den.
They shall not hurt nor destroy in all my holy mountain;
for the earth shall be full of the knowledge of the Lord,
as the waters cover the sea.

(Isaiah XI, 8-9.)

"Peace" window of the United Nations Secretariat Building. *(detail).* ⇒→

TUDELEY CHURCH

In memory of Sarah d'Avigdor Goldsmid. 1967.

Window of the chancel, 3.24×1.90 m.

Final cartoon for the Chancel window.

Tudeley: a small village in Kent, about thirty miles from London. For the first time I find myself in the English countryside. It is a clear autumn morning, with the yellow foliage of the birches enhanced by the sun. The church is made of brick and is placed between the hedges of the meadows. Its apse stands in a churchyard dotted by a few flowers, a few crosses and a few tombstones. Madame d'Avigdor Goldsmid asked Chagall to design the stained-glass window dedicated to the memory of her daughter Sarah. A few years before, both of them had admired an exhibition held in Paris of the windows destined for Jerusalem. Madame d'Avigdor Goldsmid told me how her daughter was drowned at sea with friends during a sailing accident. Before she left me to walk to her daughter's grave she said to me: *"Look at the red horse... Many people have thought that it was a reminder that my daughter was a passionate rider... But Chagall would confess that he had painted it as a token of happiness."* True enough, if the memory of the tragedy is preserved in this work, at the same time everything is striving

137

to alleviate the bereavement and the misery. The weather was so fair two days after All Saints' Day that I could not stop watching the tremulous movements of the daylight through the sprightly window. It was as if Chagall had inscribed and engraved upon it a mood of silence and solitude, not fraught with desolation or inducing despair, but, on the contrary, propitious to prayer and to the highest reaches of spiritual accomplishment. The Christ of charity here counterbalances the feeling of misery and the tears. In the center of the world, in the center of the heart, is the cross of the Passion and of the Resurrection. At the source and spring of life, everything converges toward it: the sea swells and heaves to assume the shape of heaven; a man borrows Jacob's ladder to climb nearer to the real place of love. Between the air and the water is an uninterrupted whisper. An indestructible wood feeds the flame of a perpetual dawn, and the horse, a solar messenger, burns unscathed, eager to bring in the light of the world. Each dawn renews here the promise, and should the sun be obscured for a moment by a cloud, when it is unveiled it invites us to gaze at a soaring movement in the window, that is also figured by a skylark taking flight in the neighboring field.

THE FRAUMÜNSTER, ZURICH

FIRST WINDOW :   "The Prophets Elijah, Jeremiah and Daniel." 9.76 × 0.91 m.
Signed bottom right : *Marc Chagall Reims*.

SECOND WINDOW :   "Jacob's Dream." 9.23 × 0.94 m.
Signed bottom right : *Marc Chagall 1970*.

THIRD WINDOW :   "Madonna, Child and Offering." 11.20 × 1.25 m.
Signed bottom left : *Marc Chagall Reims 1970*.

FOURTH WINDOW :   "Celestial Jerusalem." 9.23 × 0.95 m.
Signed bottom right : *Marc Chagall Reims*.

FIFTH WINDOW :   "The Prophet Isaiah's Vision on Peace and Suffering : Moses."
9.75 × 0.92 m. Signed bottom right : *Chagall Reims 1969*.

Final cartoon for the Zurich windows. ⟫⟶

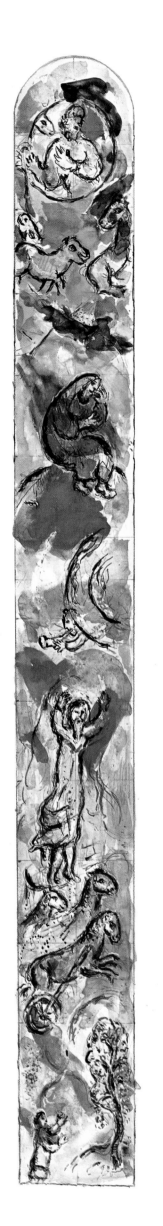

In Rheims I saw Chagall paint Christ. In Zurich I see his windows rise in a sky where sails and swans are twinkling. The Fraumünster turns its chevet toward the river and the chancel gets the first rays of daylight through five windows as slim as flutes. It is no longer summer, but it is not yet autumn. A cloudless morning; the air is damp like the iris of the eye. The five glass steles burn like firewood artfully arranged by a woodcutter who has subtly selected the various species to get differently colored flames. The twigs crackle, but no ashes soil the hearth. *Sol salutis!* Here, the highest flower in the tree is blooming, Christ whom the full orb cannot circumscribe, Christ who is the origin, who is in time and out of time. Descended into hell, dead, resurrected; after our earth plunges into each of its nights, the new sun of each day brings the earth its luminous offering, so that each dawn should be a spring and so that the regeneration of the soul through charity should be made visible in greenness.

It is the hour when the lark soars from the grass and rises with the dew toward the canopy of the sky; it is the hour when the birds join in their canticles to praise the ever-renewing light: man wakes

"Madonna, Child and Offering" window *(detail).* ⇒→

up on the first day and every tree he sees tells him of the tree of
Eden, the axle of the world, the tree of Jesse, made through Mary
the tree of the incarnation, of death and resurrection; the tree of
David that David is beholding while singing on the hills of Zion:

For thou art my lamp, O Lord;
and the Lord will lighten my darkness.

. . .

He that ruleth over men must be just,
ruling in the fear of God.
And he shall be as the light of the morning,
when the sun riseth,
even a morning without clouds;
as the tender grass springing out of the earth
by clear shining after rain.

(II Samuel XXII, 29; XXIII, 3-4.)

Bring measure into madness Chagall whispers. Such was also
the rule of the troubadours. It means to dwell musically in exalta-
tion and enthusiasm; like the sail and the hull, to come to terms
with the sea, the wind, the stars in order to succeed in the perilous
voyage. Every man who enters that place for a moment sees the
great Christ rise toward him with the sun. He sees. He sees the
beginning, he sees the present, he sees the things to come. So in
the deepest recess the spring comes to life and man, looking into
himself, lets prayer seep into him.

146

←≡ "Celestial Jerusalem" window *(detail)*.

The greatness of Chagall lies in the way he links his art to what constitutes the mysterious and mystical nature of man. He obeys the throbbings of his heart, the universal rhythms; he does not let himself be destroyed by the catastrophe, by the fall into the history of the spiritual reality; on the contrary he steeps the daily happenings into a higher history, into an immemorial tale that he must transmit as a witness, just as have done the greatest poets, the true artists, starting with the anonymous builders of temples and churches, the mosaic makers, the painters of frescoes and icons, up to El Greco, Rembrandt, Poussin, Delacroix, and others in times closer to us.

Chagall also said: *The poet always uses the same vocabulary, but he writes different poems.* That is the reason why there is not any break in Chagall's work. Here we see again Elijah and Elisha, Jeremiah, the angel with the shofar, Jacob, the ladder and the celestial travellers, David the Psalmist, Moses and the Tables of the Law, the serpent, the horse, Isaiah and the six-winged cherubim. The flames which carried the revealed word flicker up and down in long wreaths: the painter inscribes and engraves, his hand obeys his breath, the breathing of his body and of his soul. All traces of his labor have disappeared, grace emerges, the work is transmuted into song: the first rays, which in Jerusalem glitter in the blues and the yellows of Reuben, Simeon, Levi, are in Zurich, a few hours later, the harbingers of spring in the window of Christ, and when the shadows are already lengthening in the East, in Pocantico Hills they are still the fire which sets the prophets ablaze, which burns or holds up the prophets aloft.

CHAGALL
IN THE RHEIMS WORKSHOP

←─◄ "Madonna, Child and Offering" window *(detail)*.

Technique is merely the way that an artist handles his material, and it is the finished work which lets his treatment be apparent. There is no pre-established technique for a given work, and the first mosaics, the first frescoes, the first stained-glass windows are no less perfect than those which succeeded them. The painter is aware of no borderline between art and craftsmanship, and all our work with Marc Chagall is summed up in this common effort to invent constantly and always avoid being caught in the process of translation.

Marc Chagall, possibly similar to some early Renaissance painter in this respect, has the talent to inspire the members of his team. Far from asking them to be faithful to his model (in itself a work of art, and impossible to duplicate), he mysteriously incites you to experience anew his act of creation through the medium of another art. And the love he expects us to share is, as we know, full of cogency, more powerful than the best possible intentions.

151

One of our first conversations comes to my mind. Chagall had just been commissioned by Robert Renard to make the Metz windows. After doing the two small Assy windows, he now had to fathom the boundless and colorful space of a gothic cathedral. We discussed the orientation of the windows, the way shapes are altered in a gothic building, but above all we talked about what happens when the light crosses the window, at every moment on the verge of disrupting it, magnifying the radiation of the tones, transforming the shapes according to their transparency or their opacity, holding last but not least a sovereign sway over forms and colors. We never mentioned technical questions, leading, scaling of glass...; lifeless frameworks in which life itself would have withered away. Chagall was entirely wrapt up in his vision, waiting until he was actually at work to discover its artistic shape.

A little while later, in front of the large models of the windows, I experienced the same feeling. How was it possible to be faithful to the modulation, the luminous song of the coloring? A thousand difficulties, even some impossibilities, assailed my mind. But I was only listening to this urge to create, to this fiery need to give birth to the vision of the painter.

Back in my workshop, I tried scales of tones, looking henceforth to impart to the glass this resilience, this flowing continuity of the light. I was gradually led to have made a whole series of flashed glass, which would permit a modulation of tone in the core of the same glass. Bu means of acid etching you can thus obtain a scaling of values in the same tone down to the point of the emergence of a pure white in the color, and this can be done wihout making use of the transitional effect of the black setting provided by the leading. The ability to see this light is for me the very life of the stained-glass window, for it is the white that makes colors alive, determines them, defines them, limiting the optical blending and, throughout, fulfilling the function of a transitional tone, the way black does when grisaille is used.

His cartoon—the working proposition provided by the painter—ready, Chagall is expecting my own proposition, this time in terms of glass and cames. And when he says: *Now show me what you can do,* what he has in mind are the demands of freedom, his faith in the ability of our poor hands, with the help of God, to let the creative act take place. He shows us humbly that his genius is greater than he is, great enough to inspire others.

How I admire his way of grasping what is beyond him when he comes into the workshop. My work is there—a stained-glass window in which every detail is of great importance for him, but for which he is not yet responsible. With what power he penetrates this new reality that is scattered, gasping for words, reduced to its skeleton. *I take it whole,* as he says, not bothering with minor objections, aware that he can take all those forms, all those colors which are still alien to him, and make them his. He harmonizes the glasses, examining, correcting, amending only a few essential points, but with astonishing precision. It is possible that his love for France is very much the result of the clarity of thought it brings to him in his flights into the irrational.

Trial pane for the window of "The Tribe of Joseph" for the Hadassah
Medical Center Synagogue. 0.98×0.97 m. Executed May 1960.

Now the window must be "done." Using his medium like the
clay Adam was made of, the glazier has handled the glass, the masses,
the possible forms, the necessary weight of color, but the window
is still in want of the initial, vital breath, like a lifeless creature.

Then Chagall starts working under our dazzled eyes.

He comes into the workshop with the punctuality of a craftsman
who knows that only through hard work will he get anything done,

Trial pane for the window of "The Tribe of Zebulun" for the Hadassah
Medical Center Synagogue. 0.96 × 1.04 m. Executed May 1960.

and sometimes with the precision of those tightrope-walkers who delight him and who, up in the air, gracefully fly in a weightless atmosphere by dint of considerable daily exertion.

He is a craftsman who comes to life when he come in contact with his material, as if he was dealing with flowers, or poets, or ordinary men. This material, he says, *is a talisman... to handle this talisman is a matter of feeling*. The abstract idea always says too much or too little, and with him the intellect must remain outside the workshop door.

In the soul there is some intelligence, but in the intelligence there is not always a soul.

He is painting. The grisaille, through the sole impact of the line and of the value, allows him now to justify all...

With him, form comes straight from his soul. There is no idea in it, no symbol, not even any reminiscence. I watch this particular curve becoming, according to the mood, a plant, a flower, a face, an animal, the moon... or remain just a mere curve. Intense concentration results in a new form springing forth. The limits of both measure and excess are infinite. He gazes, builds up the distances from the very center of his stroke of brush, rejects the impulse, starts again, mysteriously painting his way toward a new image that he does not yet know.

The way he feels his subject suggests a line, a brush stroke, and this stroke makes him grasp his subject more clearly. Painting makes the painter see.

In this constant back and forth movement, the window takes shape and gradually finds its particular form. What matters is not the subject, or the technique, or the feelings, or even the sensibility of the painter, but only a mysterious agreement between the light and the eye, between the grisaille and the hand, between space and time, a kind of biological, molecular agreement that is made visible in the rhythm, the color and the proportions. And just when the glass seems to have been infused with its exact weight of grisaille, its right amount of life, the painter's hand stops as if another hand were holding it back. But any form which has not been nourished by the painter's blood is doomed to die, to wilt, to fade away, to dissolve.

Chagall mentions chemistry... There is no need to step back in order to be able to see; a particular stroke brings the whole painting into focus, a single pane of glass reveals the whole window. All is self-contained, all is present in each point of a living work. A stroke is conceived in a twinkling; it is the product of millions of year of accumulated energy, of the slow ripening of a gesture ceaselessly repeated, like obscurely maturing sedimentary strata. *Look at Rembrandt, look at Chardin, look at Monet, each one has his own chemistry.*

How then is it possible to speak about technique when for him the *how to do* is understood in terms of *how to be*? How can I talk logically when I see the sublime fatigue of work abolish all will and hand the creator over to *color, light, freedom*?

Color... The passionate density of red, the infinite interchanges of blue, the great repose of green, the sombre mystery of violet, the implacable limitations of yellow... Color is here brought to the plenitude of its wealth, and Chagall loves that kind of color. But his own color is something different.

Oh! That's not the coloring. It's not a matter of blue and red in that... Find your color and you've found your way. His grisaille spreads in sheets, works through accents, and through its values it imparts order and harmony, until the moment when the musical quality of the color-sensation can be perceived.

Light... *Either you kill it or it kills you, and that is not the way to deal with it.* This light which flows through the work to be painted, which animates it and makes it alive, you first have to tame it, direct it, keep it enclosed in the glass, let it live in its own right place.

To make a stained-glass window is not such an easy thing. You must catch it like you catch a mouse. Not in a cage, but with your hand. There are no tricks ; it is hit or miss.

Chagall scrapes, washes, repaints, gets angry.

What a nightmare ; you must fight with the leading, fight on and on, and then perhaps, you get what you want.

Oh ! I don't know to draw... You musn't know how to draw... A line is something that the good Lord can draw perfectly. When X... or Y... do it, it is still a line, but the Lord is no longer in it. Then I make little dots, stipples, like this, full of little unimportant things...

His hand runs over the glass, leaving behind splotches, lines, washes, claw marks, fingerprints... for a full hour...

Oh ! I've forgotten everything. Where am I?

Freedom... an instant always starting afresh. Childhood is his source and his purpose; childhood, from which he came fully grown, from which he still takes everything. As a painter he is still a new-born babe. His anguish, his torments, his long life of work have made him hoary, but for him painting begins with the rising light.

The test of the masterpiece is its freshness.

He has freshness of Mozart and of Schubert, whom he ecstatically enjoys and who restore his powers after long hours of work.

A quartet by Schubert... *Art must be like that. Ah! Schubert, he wept because he had no friends, no love, nothing; but he overturned the world. Listen to the way he weeps... I like it... Ah! How much he has suffered.*

He works, grows tender and thinks aloud...

A quintet by Mozart... *Where did he manage to get that? Somebody whispered it to him... sing that... sing that... and he sings, he listens to the dictation of the angels... That is not within everyone's reach. He can do whatever he wants, on the right, on the left... it works, it works...*

Chagall goes on building up his work, and his craft goes alongside. And, in the dazzling light of the creation I am unable to distinguish the latter from the former.

The poet's dream of a subject matter that is forever new and luminous is perhaps what impels him to leave so hurriedly what he has just finished, to find the street again and the life outside where tomorrow he can see a new form spring into life.

CHARLES MARQ

THIS VOLUME DEVOTED TO THE STAINED
GLASS WINDOWS EXECUTED BY CHAGALL
UP TO 1970 WAS COMPLETED IN FEBRUARY 1973
ON THE PRESSES OF THE IMPRIMERIE UNION
AND OF MOURLOT FRÈRES IN PARIS.
IT WAS BOUND BY RELBRO IN MALAKOFF